NUT CRACKING ON THE G.W.R.

RAILWAY
RIBALDRY

MR. W. HEATH ROBINSON'S OWN PRIVATE RAILWAY ENGINE, NOT OFTEN ALLOWED
ON THE G.W.R.

RAILWAY RIBALDRY

BEING 96 PAGES OF
RAILWAY HUMOUR

BY
W·HEATH
ROBINSON

THE STOWAWAY

FIRST PUBLISHED BY THE GREAT WESTERN RAILWAY
PADDINGTON STATION, W.2.

[James Milne, General Manager]

IN THE CENTENARY YEAR OF THE COMPANY

1935

4

A BROAD-GAUGE ENGINE DRIVER FRATERNISING WITH
A NARROW-GAUGE ENGINE DRIVER AFTER AN
AMICABLE SETTLEMENT OF THE DISPUTE

FOREWORD

—

THE GREAT WESTERN RAILWAY celebrates its one hundredth birthday this year, but unlike other centenarians such as trees and turtles, grows more youthful after a century of existence.

The Company, serious in its determination to maintain the enviable reputation that it has acquired in the past, is, as will be seen in the pages that follow, not without a sense of humour in giving Mr. W. Heath Robinson a free hand to apply his skill to the portrayal of certain events in its history.

Occasional excursions in a lighter vein help us to take life a little less seriously than we are generally called upon to do. It is hoped therefore that this contribution to the library of humour will be appreciated by our patrons, present and to be.

THE FIRST DOG'S TICKET

LIST OF DRAWINGS

VIGNETTES

THE RED FLAG

A WELL THOUGHT OUT AND NEARLY SUCCESSFUL
EXPERIMENT BY EARLY RAILWAY PIONEER

EARLY RAILWAY PIONEERS PROSPECTING FOR A SITE FOR A TERMINUS BY
THE UPPER REACHES OF THE PADDINGTON CANAL

THE OFFICIAL WATER DIVINER OF THE COMPANY MAKING SURE THAT THERE IS
WATER IN THE BOILER BEFORE THE COMMENCEMENT OF A LONG RUN

11

BUILDING THE FIRST LOCOMOTIVE

A VERY OLD BUT EFFICIENT TEST FOR BRAKES

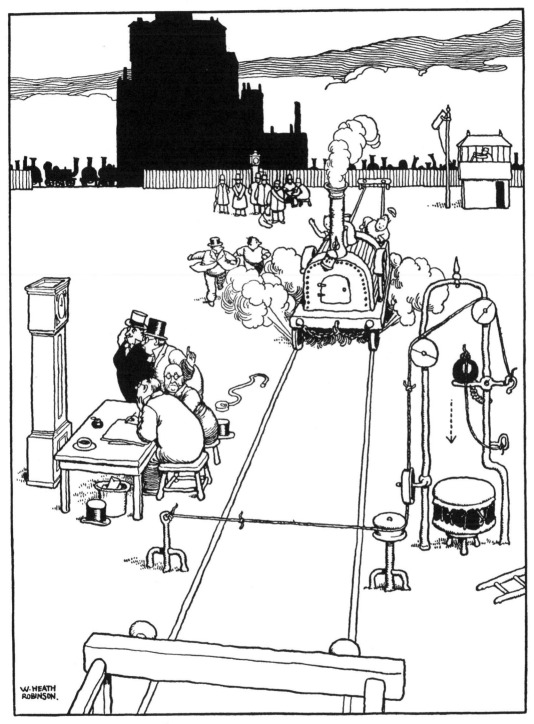

AN OLD-FASHIONED METHOD OF TESTING THE SPEED OF ENGINES

14

CHECKING THE FIRST TIME-TABLE BEFORE PUBLICATION

INGENIOUS PLAN FOR FIXING THE APPROXIMATE TIMES FOR TRAINS
TO COVER THE REQUIRED DISTANCE, USED SUCCESSFULLY IN THE
COMPLETION OF THE FIRST TIME-TABLE

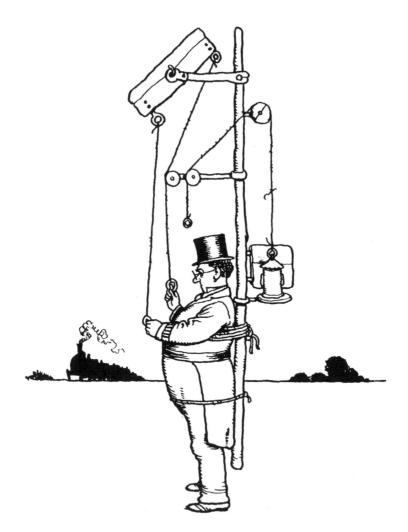

AN EARLY AND INTERESTING TYPE OF SIGNAL

NIGHT DUTY AT ONE OF THE FIRST RAILWAY SIGNALS

AN ERROR OF JUDGMENT IN THE GOODS YARD

GOODS AND PASSENGERS CARRIED TOGETHER IN THE OPEN

20

A SIMPLE METHOD OF DEALING WITH THE SMOKE
NUISANCE IN THE DAYS OF THE OPEN CARRIAGE

21

BORING THE FIRST TUNNEL WITH AN EARLY TYPE OF ROTARY EXCAVATOR

AN UNFORTUNATE START FOR THE SUMMER HOLIDAYS

PULLING THE COMMUNICATION CORD IN ONE OF THE OLD OPEN CARRIAGES

PUTTING THE FINISHING TOUCHES AFTER A GOOD
CLEAN UP

EARLY METHODS OF ENGINE CLEANING

THE RAILWAY POLICEMAN SAVES THE SITUATION

VARIED DUTIES OF RAILWAY POLICE

28

A SIMPLE DEVICE FOR PREVENTING RAILWAY POLICEMEN FROM
BEING RUN DOWN WHEN WALKING THE LINE

W·HEATH ROBINSON

A VERY EARLY TYPE OF MECHANICAL SIGNAL, NOW RARELY TO BE SEEN!

BEFORE THERE WERE ANY WAITING-ROOMS

THE FIRST WAITING-ROOM

A LITTLE RELAXATION BY THE WAY

THE FIRST EXCURSION TRAIN

34

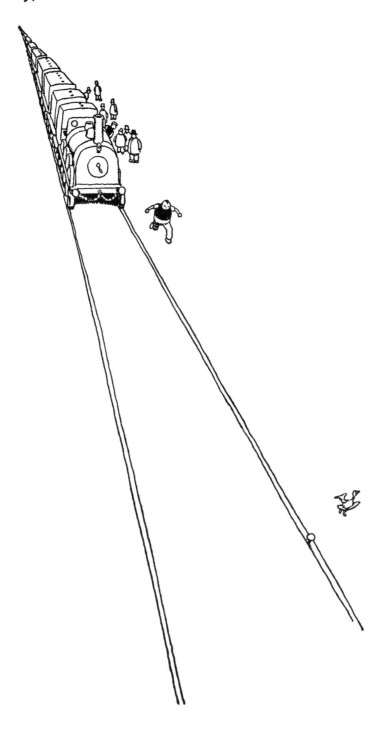

"WASTE NOT, WANT NOT"
IS THE DRIVER'S MOTTO

INSTALLING THE ELECTRIC TELEGRAPH BETWEEN PADDINGTON AND SLOUGH

ONE OF THE EARLIEST HONEYMOON TRAINS RUN BY THE G.W.R.

A PICTURESQUE CEREMONY—THE MAYOR IN STATE LETTING THROUGH THE
FIRST TRAIN IN A NEW RAILWAY STATION

AN EARLY EXPERIMENT BY THE INVENTOR
OF THE ATMOSPHERIC SYSTEM

THE FIRST "LADIES ONLY" COMPARTMENT

THE ATMOSPHERIC PRINCIPLE AS APPLIED TO SIGNALS
IN THE FIRST ATMOSPHERIC RAILWAY

A NEARLY SUCCESSFUL EFFORT TO INTRODUCE THE ATMOSPHERIC SYSTEM
OF TRACTION

THE KIND OF THING WE WERE SOMETIMES REDUCED
TO BEFORE THE INTRODUCTION OF FOOT WARMERS

43

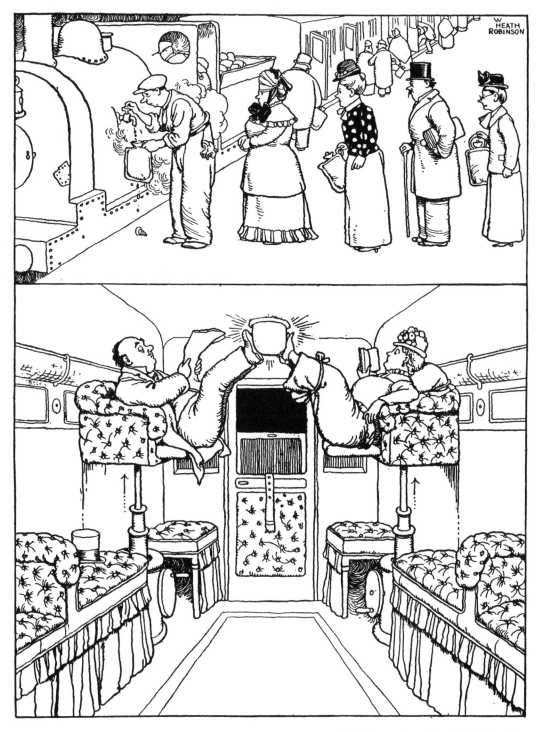

INTERESTING METHOD OF OVERCOMING THE "COLD FEET" DIFFICULTY BEFORE THE
INTRODUCTION OF FOOT WARMERS

SECTIONAL VIEW OF THE INTERIOR OF THE FIRST
AUTOMATIC MACHINE

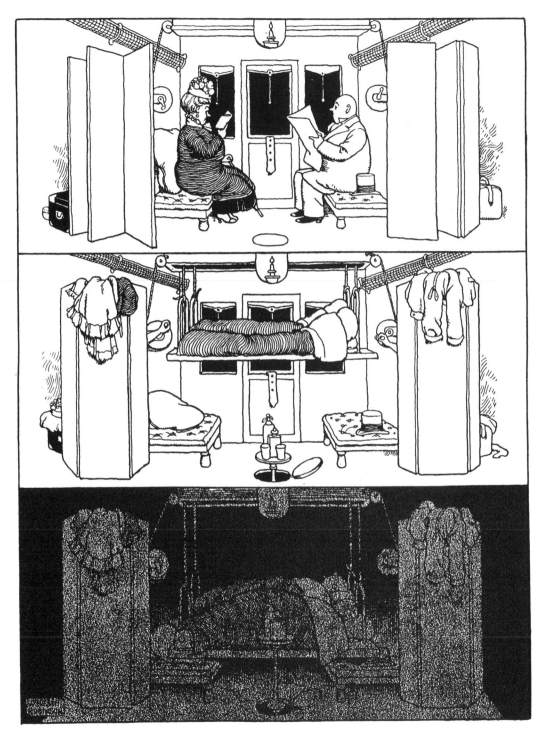

THE FIRST SLEEPING COMPARTMENT

THE SORT OF THING LIKELY TO
INTERFERE WITH THE SMOOTH
RUNNING OF THE SERVICE

AN ANTIQUATED METHOD OF FILLING THE BOILERS WITHOUT STOPPING THE ENGINE
BEFORE THE INTRODUCTION OF THE WATER-TROUGH SYSTEM

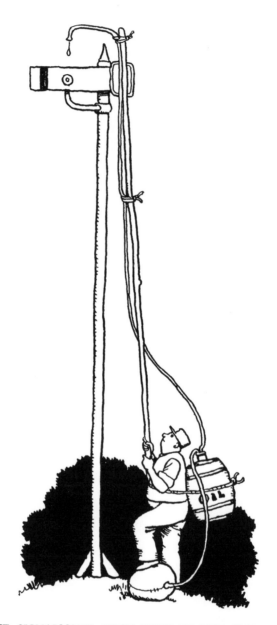

THE SIGNALMAN'S FIRST DUTY IN THE MORNING—
OILING THE SIGNAL

THE COMPANY STARTS STEAMER SERVICES

THE SORT OF THING THAT SOME-
TIMES HAPPENS WHEN CARELESSLY
LOOKING OVER BRIDGES

THE BUILDING OF SALTASH BRIDGE

JUST IN TIME

THE LAST POST FOR THE COUNTRY—AN EARLY ATTEMPT AT PICKING UP
MAILS WITHOUT STOPPING

A SIMPLE DEVICE ENABLING SMOKERS TO SMOKE IN NON-SMOKING COMPARTMENTS WITHOUT ANNOYANCE TO THE OTHER PASSENGERS

THE FIRST SMOKING CARRIAGE

LIGHTING UP BEFORE ENTERING A TUNNEL

SECTIONAL VIEW OF THE EXCAVATIONS FOR THE SEVERN TUNNEL, SHOWING THE HARD
AND FOSSILIFEROUS NATURE OF THE GROUND TO BE PENETRATED

58

THE ADJUSTABLE CHIMNEY TO FIT ANY SIZE TUNNEL

AN EARLY TYPE OF ENGINE FOR CLEANING TUNNELS

INGENIOUS DEVICE FOR RUNNING A NARROW
GAUGE ENGINE ON BROAD GAUGE TRACK

THE CHANGE OVER FROM BROAD TO NARROW GAUGE

OLD AGE

NEW USES FOR OLD RAILWAY ENGINES

A BUSMAN'S HOLIDAY

THE KIND-HEARTED ENGINE DRIVER

THE FIRST BATHING COMPARTMENT

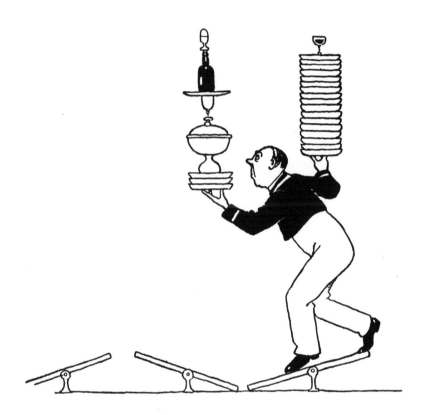

TRAINING RESTAURANT CAR ATTENDANT TO CARRY ON
DURING UNCERTAIN MOTION OF TRAIN

HOW THEY TEACH YOUNG ENGINE DRIVERS THE MEANING OF THE SIGNALS

THE ABSENT-MINDED MAN WHO COULD
NOT FIND HIS TICKET

TRAINING MEMBERS OF THE STAFF TO CLOSE
THE CARRIAGE DOORS WHEN THE TRAIN IS IN MOTION

TRAINING TICKET COLLECTORS

W. HEATH ROBINSON

TRAINING THE STAFF

CONSTERNATION OF PASSENGERS IN FIRST SLIP CARRIAGE

HOW THEY TRAIN RAILWAY PORTERS TO MANŒUVRE THEIR LOADS ON
CROWDED PLATFORMS

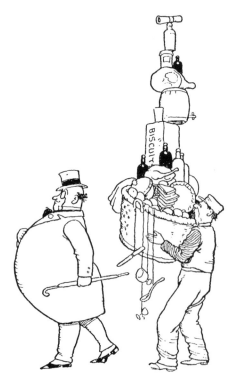

THE FIRST LUNCHEON BASKET

TAKING SEATS FOR LUNCH ON ONE OF THE FIRST TRAINS TO BE EQUIPPED WITH
RESTAURANT CARS

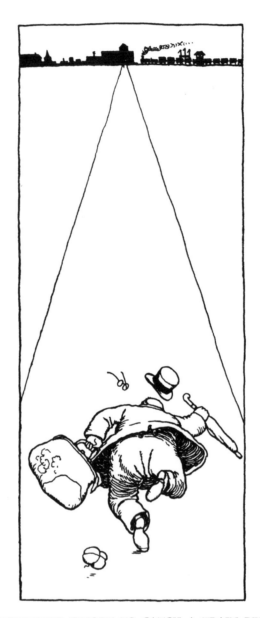

A CREDITABLE EFFORT TO CATCH A TRAIN BEFORE
THE ERA OF THE RAILWAY MOTOR BUS

THE FIRST RAILWAY BUS

BOLD MOVE IN THE CAMPAIGN TO
DO AWAY WITH RAILWAY PORTERS

OLD GENTLEMAN RECOGNISING HIS LOST UMBRELLA IN THE BROLLY DEPARTMENT
OF THE LOST PROPERTY OFFICE

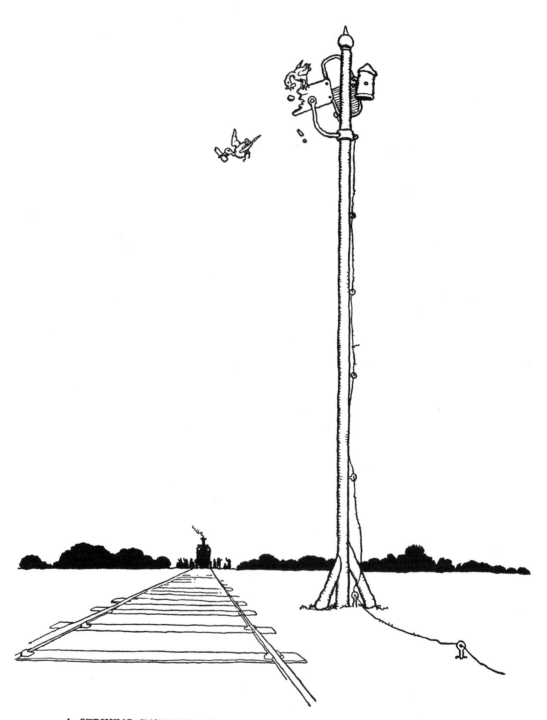

A STRIKING INSTANCE OF THE RAVAGES OF THE WILD WOODPECKER

RELIEVING THE TEDIUM OF WAITING FOR THE SIGNAL ON THE SLOW TRAIN—
BETWEEN PADDINGTON AND LAND'S END VIA SOUTHAMPTON, HEREFORD
AND WESTON-SUPER-MARE

TOO LATE! A PATHETIC ATTEMPT TO ARREST THE PROGRESS OF THE RECORD
BREAKING PLYMOUTH-LONDON TRAIN, MAY 9TH, 1904

A SPEED OF 102 M.P.H. CAUSES A STIR IN RAILWAY CIRCLES

OFF TO IRELAND VIA FISHGUARD AND ROSSLARE

BEFORE THE ADVENT OF G.W.R. TURBINE STEAMERS
ON THE FISHGUARD-ROSSLARE ROUTE TO IRELAND

84

INGENIOUS CONTRIVANCE FOR PICKING UP THE DRIVER'S BREAKFAST
WITHOUT STOPPING THE TRAIN

THE NEW HUMANE COW-CATCHER

PASSENGERS WAITING FOR THE TRAIN IN THE
FLOODED DISTRICTS

HOW THEY NEGOTIATED THE FLOODED DISTRICTS IN THE SHORT CUT TO THE WEST

POPULARITY OF THE HIKERS' MYSTERY EXPRESS LEADS TO
THE SAME IDEA ON THE ROAD

THE FIRST HIKERS' MYSTERY EXPRESS ARRIVES

THE END OF THE SEASON!

THE G.W.R. TAKES TO THE AIR

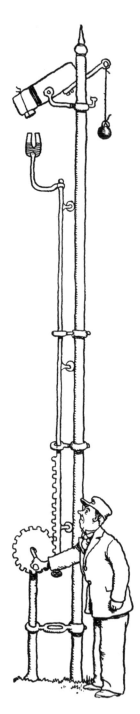

THE FIRST MAGNETIC SIGNAL

ONE OF THE MANY SUGGESTIONS FOR DOING WITHOUT TUNNELS

WHEN COAL WAS CHEAP

A NOT INFREQUENT CAUSE OF DELAY IN THE PICTURESQUE DISTRICTS OF THE
WEST OF ENGLAND

THE END

Published in Great Britain in 2016 by Old House books & maps
c/o Osprey Publishing, PO Box 883, Oxford OX2 9PH, UK.
c/o Osprey Publishing, PO Box 3985, New York, NY 10185-3985, USA.
Website: www.oldhousebooks.co.uk

A CIP catalogue record for this book is available from the British Library.

ISBN-13: 978 1 90840 294 3

Originally published in 1935 by the Great Western Railway, London.

Printed in China through Worldprint Ltd.

16 17 18   10 9 8 7 6 5 4 3